OTHER BOOKS IN THE SERIES:

Over 50s' Jokes   **Over 60s' Jokes**

Over 70s' Jokes   **Over 80s' Jokes**

Golf Jokes

OTHER BOOKS BY HELEN EXLEY:

365 Happy Days!   **Live! Laugh! Love!**

Life! And other disasters...   **Senior Moments 365**

The little book of Gratitude   **Be You!**

Published in 2019 by Helen Exley ®London in Great Britain.
Design, selection and arrangement © Helen Exley Creative Ltd 2019.
Illustrated by Roland Fiddy © Helen Exley Creative Ltd 2019.
All the words by Pam Brown copyright © Helen Exley Creative Ltd 2019.
The moral rights of the authors have been asserted.

12 11 10 9 8 7 6 5 4 3 2 1

ISBN: 978-1-78485-236-8

**Helen Exley ® London,
16 Chalk Hill, Watford, Herts WD19 4BG, UK
www.helenexley.com**

Cat
Jokes

WRITTEN BY PAM BROWN
ILLUSTRATIONS BY ROLAND FIDDY
EDITED BY HELEN EXLEY

Helen Exley

Cat owner?
Mistress?
Master?
Nothing
applies.
Slave
comes near it.

Cats don't live with you,
cats board with you.

Some people have Mug
written across their forehead.
Recognised by any cat
needing a service.

I love you.
I adore you.
You are at the heart
of my life,
says Dog.
Of course I love you.
Where's dinner?
says Cat.

Fussy

Only a beginner
buys a crate
of Tabby's Top Food.
They have not yet
understood
the passion lasts a week.
After which to offer it
is an insult.

Every cat owner
has the temptation
to tie a little purse
around their pussy's neck
and send it down
to the supermarket
to choose what it's prepared
to eat this week.

All cats
are beautiful –
even the
ugly ones.

A cat is
a small
perfection.

One feels
totally
grateful
to be
owned
by a cat.

A great many cats have,
unknown to their
official owners, several names –
given by suckers
who have been hoodwinked
into believing they are
sad little strays.

A cat obeys

A cat can always
out-think you.

A lost dog is a pitiable,
bewildered creature.
Poor soul.
A lost cat
is looking for an
alternative residence.

rules. His.

People, in exasperation,
sometimes wonder
whether they
own their cats,
or their cats
own them.
The cats do not need
to speculate.

"Come" says master –
and the cat sits.
"Go" he says –
and the cat stays.
Use your entire vocabulary
on a cat and he will do exactly
as he pleases.

Cats assure us
that we are not gods.

A cat believes in privacy
His.
Not yours.
It is a very good thing
that a cat cannot voice
his opinions.

A cat begins the night
at the end of your bed.
By morning
he has taken possession
and you are on the edge.

There is nothing

A cat has his priorities.
If you are very lucky
you come second.

A cat is deeply offended
if asked to shift himself.
He expects a polite request.
Though, of course,
he does not intend to move,
even then.

so obstinate
as an obstinate cat.

A cat will vividly
enact the chase
with a dry leaf as a mouse
– until some
silly human being says,
"Kill it. Kill the mouse!"
When he will stare
in disdain,
"Mouse?
For heavens sake,
can't you see
it's a dead leaf!"

Humans are idiots

A cat is often
exasperated by the
dim-wittedness of humans,
but lives in hope
that with time,
patience and affection,
it will be able to instil
a little sense into them.

If Cat wants to sleep
anywhere he will.
Your chair, the lettuce bed,
the kitchen stove,
the airing cupboard,
the sink.
Your head.

A cat has mastered
conservation of energy.
If nothing demands his
immediate attention
– he simply switches off.

You are
mistaken,
says Cat.
This is
my chair.

Never believe anything

One always finds one's cat
is adept at opening cabinets.
Too late.

A cat can out-think
and out-manoeuvre
any human being.

is out of a cat's reach.

Fiddy

A BORED CAT IS AN INVENTIVE CAT.

A bored cat is an inventive cat.
Vincent passed the time
in throwing things.
Clocks. Vases. Ornaments and
telephones. Remote controls and pens.
However high. However tricky.
With age he seems to have given it up,
but sometimes, rarely,
he focuses with an expression
of concentrated glee,
angles a paw and flings something
to the carpet.
It's good to see
there's life in the old cat yet.

A cat ignores
expensive gifts
of toys.
Preferring a walnut,
a Brussels sprout,
a bit of string,
a toilet roll
or an
exceedingly
tiny mouse.

A cat has
a very short
attention span
unless
he's waiting
at a mouse hole.

No cat
is ever guilty

A kitten can
and will fall off
almost anything.
But will never admit
it was an accident.

No, says Cat.
I was nowhere near the kippers.
At any time.

A cat
who has
broken
something
swears
he was
never
near
the
thing.

To possess a cat
is to be a part
of a world-wide company
of devoted slaves.

How airily our cats
summon and dismiss us.
And we obey.

The smallest kitten
only needs a week
to be in total charge
of a home
and its owners.

At best, one is one's cat's
companion.
At worst, a weak
and pathetic servant.

You may
love me,
says cat.
On my terms.

Try dominating a cat, and he'll leave home.

A cat never entirely forgets his ancestry. He feels entitled to respect.

Your cat the

When your cat stands
and stares at you he is asking
to go out,
to have his litter changed,
to be given his supper,
to change the water in his bowl,
boss!   to play,
to have a little conversation.
Or simply to inform you that it's time
for everyone to go to bed.
He is making his request
perfectly clear.

All over the world
people are sitting,
or lying,
in extreme
discomfort
rather than
disturb the cat.

To be cut dead by your cat
means you are guilty
of some heinous crime.
Usually he does not tell you what,
but leaves you to work it out.

People spend
a lot of time apologising
to their cats.

Every now and
again your cat
will take the
Egyptian Pose.
Just to remind you
he's a god.

A cat will play with
the string you are dangling
with infinite skill and total
concentration – until,
within half a second, he stops,
stares and walks away.
"Now I've indulged you
long enough.
I have better things to do."
And you are left alone
with your piece of string.

Kit,

Katten,

Cat.

Charm.

Mischief.

Wisdom.

A cat means
to do everything
with elegance
and is horribly
embarrassed
if he fails.

Come to your call?
says cat.
Don't be ridiculous.
I have my self-respect.

A cat hates
above any
other thing
making
a fool of
itself.

It takes a lot of
judicious stroking
before your cat is willing
to forgive you
any sin.

Any competent psychiatrist
confronted with analysis
of a feline mind
would be driven
to retirement
after a single session.

A cat has no hesitation
on complaining of your treatment
with utter conviction
to a member of the family.
With no justification whatsoever.
– He didn't like his dinner.
Or you didn't switch off the rain.

You might presume
I love you,
says Cat.
But not at this
precise moment.
I am otherwise
occupied.

Even the most
affectionate cat needs time
to himself.
"Of course I love you.
But go away."

A cat
co-operates
as long as
it suits him.

Dear human,
you believe
you know
what I am
thinking
– but you
never do.

A cat can pretend
that a moving light,
a piece of string,
a fallen leaf,
or its tail
is a mouse.
Until a human says,
playfully,
"Kill that mousy then!"
When it is met
with a withering stare.

A cat knows very well
what Go. Come. Stay mean.
He simply refuses
to acknowledge them
as applying to himself.
A cat gives instructions.
He does not take them.

Disobedient

No one has ever
owned a cat.

The words No!
Get Down!
Stop!
Leave it!
Mean nothing
to a cat.

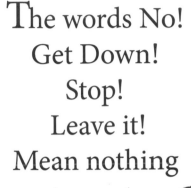

A cat is always
on the wrong side
of any door.

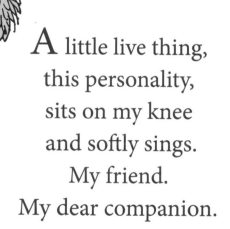

A little live thing,
this personality,
sits on my knee
and softly sings.
My friend.
My dear companion.

A cat does not leap up at you,
or lick your face
all over or run mad circles
round you,
making hysterical noises.
It meets you at the door
and leans very softly
against your legs
and reverberates.

"Slow down" says Cat.
Sit here with me
and stroke my fur
and I will sing your
tensions clean away.

Here, Mum!
Wake up!
See what
I've brought you.
I've put it on
your pillow.
Look!
A most lovely snail!

Five mice in a row.
I love to show my gratitude.
They are a gift,
just for you.

I am old,
says Cat.
I am prepared
to show you
where the
mice are.
From then on,
it's up to you.
Love you lots.

Kittens take us in hand
very soon in their lives.
They summon us to play.
They sulk if put down from our knees.
They hog the bed.

Feed me, stroke me, scratch me,
says the cat.
Arrange amusements!

So – you're back.
But don't expect a greeting.
I'll sit here and exude reproach,
Disappointment, Umbrage.
No.
Sardines won't do.
No. I will not be chirruped at and cajoled.
… Haddock?
That's different.
I will relax the reprimand.
Just a little.
– But don't do it again.

Albert moved in
after having explored
the possibilities
of most
other houses
in the street.
Good garden,
a women who
was obviously
a kindly,
easily persuaded
mug.

The best thing
that God
ever did
for kittens,
was to invent
string.

"No. Not that dish.
Too big.
And plastic.
Find another please.
China. Small.
There, by the door.
Not too near the wall.
That's right.
Now, get the fork
and spread it around a bit.
Fine.
Now go away
and leave me to my meal."

"Look! It's your special treat!"
"What? That?
Not me.
You must be mistaken."
And Mog walks away, offended.

Cat has always known
his lineage was
more distinguished
than any Pharaoh.
And has lived
his life accordingly.

A cat
expects
to be
adored.

Cat owners sometimes
have an ugly suspicion
that the Lord
of the Universe
has whiskers
and a long ginger tail.

There
is nothing
in this
world
as wet as a
Wet Cat.

If a cat is Disgusted,
it's no good tempting it
with a twitching string.
You are inviting a look of
withering disdain that would
sit well on a Duchess.

A sulking cat is

"No" is not a word
that no cat can understand.

Mankind strives
for perfection.
The cat is
complacent.
He feels
he has achieved it
long ago.

solid sulk.

CALLING FOR CAT

Call a dog
and he comes.
Call a cat
and he
just may come.
Eventually.

I call into the night.
He sits in shadow and listens.
Appreciating my anxiety.
Biding his time.

Cats like to lie
and listen to you calling.
When discovered,
they are indignant
"Me? I never knew
you meant me!"

I have been calling the cat
for twenty minutes.
He is sitting three yards from you
in the shelter of a bush.
Amused.

Every cat a

A cat knows you are Going Away.
And takes umbrage.
And cats do umbrage very well.

Cats know,
quietly and with
complete conviction.
that they are
the superior species.

critic.

A cat expects a chair
at the dinner table.
Especially if it's formal.

Dog and Horse
were seen as Useful
and so were disciplined
to fit Man's needs.
Cat took no notice
and remains
simply and everlastingly
Himself.

Put a pill into a cat's mouth
successfully and stroke its throat
to make it swallow.
– After a short pause it will spit it out,
unharmed.

Cats
have
never yet
grasped
the concept
of
No.

LORD OF THE UNIVERSE

Live by
his rules
and you
and the cat
will get along
very well.

"Mum,
I've told you
four times now
to turn the
rain off.
I Am Disappointed
and angry."

No cat explains what he wants.
He expects you to understand
and work it out.

If all else fails,
standing four foot square
on your owner's face
will rouse them
to give you breakfast.

Best ask his owner
if you can pat his dog.
With cat, ask the cat.

Every cat is convinced

After scolding one's cat
one looks into its face
and is seized
by the ugly suspicion
that it understood
every word.
And has filed it
for reference.

he knows best.

The Boss!

I need to go out. Now

I am not a pet,
says Cat.
I am a person.
Acknowledge it.

There is no such thing
as a cat owner.

Fast – Or else.

Other creatures
serve humanity.
The Cat is served.

It looks
all right.
It smells
all right.
Cat says it's off.
That's it.

What a cat wants, he

People new to cats bulk-buy.
Not realising he will eat
the first four tins in rapture
and then renounce the rest forever.

At last, a cat food
he's prepared to eat.
Buy a crate.
He'll never touch it again.

invariably gets.

CLAWS

Do not confuse
the implements
in your cat's feet
with simple claws.
They are excavators,
stilettos, slings, lancets,
rippers of curtains,
engravers of furniture.

Resign yourself.
You can have
a cat
or posh furniture.

A cat believes in adding texture
to upholstery.

No, says Cat.
The fact
the curtain linings
are in ribbons
is nothing
to do with me.

Cross kitten!

"Missis.
Look into my eyes.
Be honest.
Would you willingly
go out
in a heavy frost
and wee
in the evergreen?"

Fail to turn off
the rain
– and be held
accountable.

A cross kitten
comes across the room,
burning with rage –
his fur on end.
At all costs
do not laugh at him.
A kitten has his pride.

Cats,
you must
realise,
have quietly
taken over
the world.

A cat acknowledges

Those who
require
obedience
should not
acquire
a cat.

no Superior Being.

A cat can clear
a plate of food
and leave the pill
you had
disguised
naked in
the middle.

No cat is as virtuous

A dog
looks
guilty
if he's
sinned.
A cat,
never.

as he looks.

Fall flat in the kitchen
and your cat
will look up from his dinner.
"Fool" he says.
And goes on eating.

A cat can be very
pointed in his
disapproval.
Especially of visitors.

A cat can give very
precise instructions.
"A flea. Here, at my shoulder.
Fetch the comb.
Down a bit.
No. There.
Ah.
You have it.
You may withdraw."

Some cats delight in
suddenly falling on you
from a great height,
while you sleep.

One can sleep through
a thunderstorm.
Through ructions in the street.
Through low-flying jet planes.
But not through
a little cat
patting your face
with his paw.

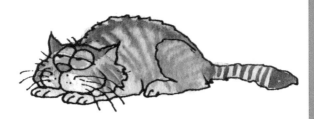

Wake in the night
to find, an inch from your nose,
two great, questioning eyes.
"There's a good boy" you say.
"Go back to sleep."
"A snack?" he says.
"No. It's half past three."

An ecstatic cat,
can purr
so loudly
it makes you
laugh out loud
with joy.

A cat does not
need to demonstrate
his affection wildly.
A leaning
against your legs.
A chirrup.
A gentle paw.
"I'm glad you're home."

A cat purring
soothes the most
troubled heart.

A cat who doesn't

I know I have always
done this or that.
What of it?
I have Changed My Mind.

I sit where I sit, says cat.
I lie where I lie.
I eat when I've a mind to
and I stay with you
according to my rules.

want to, won't.

Cats have made
a profession
of being adorable.
It pays.

A cat gives
companionship
but always
with a clause.
"I can change
my mind."

What is on
your plate
is always
more desirable
than that
on his.

Greedy

It's wonderful how far a cat can enlongate its arm when it needs to steal a roasted chicken leg.

A cat can always manage a second breakfast
– donated by the kind lady up the road.
Or a third.
Or a fourth.

A cat feels it is incumbent upon him to test the trifle.

It is no use trying to

In mid-chase she stops.
Sits. Washes her feet.
Stares at you
with disapproval.
"For heavens sake woman,"
she declares.
"Act your age."

No cat ever
makes a mistake.
He makes it perfectly clear
it was intentional.

reason with a cat.

Sleeps on the bed

When you are clinging
to the edge of the bed
in order not to disturb
your cat,
take comfort
in the thought
that all over
the night-time world
thousands are sharing
your predicament.

A cat allows you
to sleep
on the bed.
On the edge.

A cat does not have to
waken you with remonstrations.
He just sits on your chest.
Puts his nose an inch away
from yours. And breathes.

Every cat knows
that the solution
to almost
everything
is sleep.

A cat asleep and

A cat apparently thinking
deep mysterious thoughts
is probably asleep.

A cat
comfortable
is a cat
hard to shift.

comfortable

A cat
in a huff
is something
to be
reckoned
with.

Perfectly sensible people apologise to cats.

A cat is angry
when you don't understand
his perfectly clear
conversation.

A cat can wither

Every tamed cat,
a small,
amiable tyrant.

No cat is
satisfied until
he has a human
firmly beneath
his paw.

with a glance.

A cat

Nothing can wheedle
like a cat.

Now, says cat.
Time for a rub-a-dub.
Put down your book.
I'll show you
where to scratch.

wheedles

A cat
lays down terms.
It is wisest
to accept them.
A cat likes to hear
you calling him.
He sits in a bush
a yard from
your shoes –
and listens.

CALLING A CAT
THAT DOES NOT COME

A cat loves
to hear you
calling its name.
It will listen
contentedly
for an hour
at a stretch.
Of course,
it won't respond –
only listen.

USES PEOPLE

Cats are loyal as long

A dog goes on loving,
however he is treated.
A cat walks out
and finds another home.

A cat is company
when you are ill.
After all you have a duvet and
hot-water bottle,
little dainty snacks
and time to spare for stroking.

as it suits them.

People use dogs
and horses, cattle,
sheep, elephants
and camels.
Cat uses people.

Let an ancient stray
into the house
and find delight
in watching him discover
a little dish of food,
a mat, and shelter
from the rain.
His purr
will shake his bones
and bring a blessing.

To at last
be allowed to touch
most gently
the head of a
frightened stray
is a thing to lift
the heart.

A cat reasons
that if it is
raining outside
the front door
it does not follow
that it is raining
outside
the back door.

A cat is never
quite sure
whether it wants to be
In or Out.

Under
the fur
of every
pedigree cat
is a Mog.

Look out
for the
bored cat –
He'll think
of something.

A cat is never bored.
At a loose end he will
remove all the keys
from their hooks,
climb the north face
of the bookcase
or eat the rubber plant.

If you will leave a vase of roses
on the piano,
what can you expect?

Cat's claws were given to it
to hunt, to fight and climb trees,
but centuries have extended
its abilities to shin up curtains,
open doors, lift lids,
and rearrange the ornaments.

Every tiny bundle of

No machine can shred
as efficiently as a cat.

FULLY ARMED

A cat leaves its mark.
On the wallpaper,
the newel posts,
the curtains,
the lettuce bed.
And in our hearts.

ur is fully armed.

I can move home

Dear Missis
I will love you
with at least half
my heart.
The rest is reserved
for the lady next door,
who gives me
smoked salmon.

tomorrow

Human beings, with
patience and tenacity,
can be made to understand
a cat's demands.
Food. Shelter. Comfort.
Those who are kind
in disposition learn.
Those who are not should
be abandoned.
One can always find
another home.

TEMPER

The most gentle cat
has a shocking
range of
swear words in
his vocabularly.

TANTRUM

One's polite cat
in a raging temper is no longer
Puss but Puma.

A cross kitten is a sight to see.
He comes across the room sideways,
tiptoe, burning with rage –
his fur on end, his tail a bottle brush...
At all costs do not laugh at him.
A kitten has his pride.

OBEY ME!

A cat cannot speak – but he can still give orders.

One acquires
a pet.
One adjusts
to a dictator.

I am telling you something.
Look.
Read my eyes.

So, it's the *denouement*
of the series you've been
waiting for for weeks.
So,
"I want the front door opening.
Now!"

Tibs climbed the poplar.
The family called up advice.
"Back down. And take it slowly."
But Tibs faced down
and Let Go All
and hurtled to their feet
in a whirlwind of leaves and twigs.
And walked away
with slightly shaken dignity.

A cat is, in the eyes
of the doctors,
a splendid calming device,
an aid to a healthy heart
and a sound old age.
True.
If he hasn't tripped you
on the stair
– or leapt from
the darkness unexpectedly,
eyes glowing,
claws grappling your neck.
In sheer affection.

A cat needs
no words
– the touch of a little paw
– a whiskery kiss
– a drowsy purr
are enough to tell you
that he loves you.

Stop scratching your cat
for one moment and
a single paw reaches out
and reminds you
to resume.

Some cats purr
like little engines
– and some softly
reverberate.

In his purr a cat invites
the world
to share his contentment.

So – you spent
an hour arranging
your knitting.
But see what I have
achieved
in ten minutes!

One should
never
delude oneself
that something
is safely out
of the reach
of a cat.

Round, misty-blue eyes
stare desperately.
Love me, they say,
let me into your life –
so that I can begin to re-organise
your entire existence.

Human

There is nothing so
down-putting as
an exasperated kitten
who has failed
to explain
something to you,
despite putting
it in words
of one syllable.

stupidity

A cat
never
ceases
to be
astounded
by your
stupidity.

COMFORT

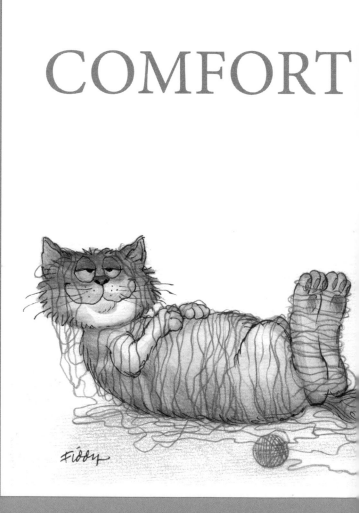

Fiddy

LOVING

He is a kindly cat,
loving beyond reason;
head-butter, nuzzler,
flubsy sprawl of fur,
belly spread,
he lies like an upturned table,
forepaws kneading,
demanding notice
and a rub-a-tum.